CW00539410

THE FAKENHAM FAVOURITE

THE STORY OF COOL ROXY & THE BLACKMORES

Aaren Gordon

Alan Blackmore

BY THE SAME AUTHOR

OUTSIDE
DESTINATION

THE FAKENHAM FAVOURITE

THE STORY OF COOL ROXY & THE BLACKMORES

AARON GRANSBY

GERARD BOOKS

First published by Gerard Books 2024

Typeset by Gerard Books

ISBN: 978-1-7394179-1-8

Published by Gerard Books, St Albans

Printed & bound by Imprint Digital, Exeter

This book is dedicated in memory of
Christopher and Michael Blackmore

Author's acknowledgements

Firstly, I would like to thank Alan and Pat Blackmore,
not only for their openness and cooperation on this book,
but also for the memories and opportunities they have given
not just me, but to so many others over the years.
I would also like to thank Chris Honour, Emily Crossman
and David Hunter for their kind and generous help.
I hope this book will be enjoyed, not just by those who
already know about the Blackmores and Cool Roxy, but by
anyone who loves and appreciates horses and the sport of
racing. Above all, I hope it does justice to the lives of two
remarkable people – and their wonderful horses.

Contents

Alan Blackmore chats with the Princess Royal at Fakenham

CHAPTER ONE

BY ROYAL APPOINTMENT

The date was 24th October 2008 and the race was the Alan Blackmore Birthday Handicap Chase at the charming Norfolk racecourse of Fakenham.

The star turn – the horse so many in the crowd had come to see – was the 11-year-old bay gelding Cool Roxy, very small for a chaser at 15.2 hands, but a specialist around the tight turns of the track where he had already won nine times.

If the horse was a veteran, so too was his owner and trainer: one A G Blackmore, whose 80th birthday the race was celebrating.

He was joined at the races, as he always was, by his wife Pat who, just one week earlier, had been given the news that she was in remission from cancer.

The couple enjoyed lunch before the race with the Princess Royal, who was attending the meeting in her role as a patron of the Injured Jockeys Fund.

Then, at 2.40pm, it was time for the main event.

Of course, running your best horse in a race named after you to mark your own 80th birthday, and with a member of the royal family watching, could have gone one of two ways.

But the result was never in doubt.

The crowd, who knew all about the Blackmores and Cool Roxy and had taken them to their hearts, cheered and cheered until the roof was in danger of coming off the stand as Roxy, with his regular jockey Chris Honour on board in the Blackmores' black and red hooped 'Dennis the Menace' colours, sailed home in splendid isolation.

He finished 24 lengths clear of the field, taking his number of wins at the track to a record-breaking 10.

Chris Honour, now a successful trainer himself, said of the day: 'It was my best day racing, by a country mile. To break the record, on Mr Blackmore's 80th birthday and with Mrs Blackmore having just been told she was in remission from cancer – you just couldn't have written it any better.

'I have ridden at the Cheltenham Festival and have since trained some very nice winners, but anything will have to go some to beat that day. It was unbelievable.'

Afterwards, to huge applause, Alan was presented with the

race winner's trophy by HRH the Princess Royal herself.

'You dream of things like this happening,' he said, 'but normally they never do. Today my dream has come true.'

That victory, in the presence of royalty, was the crowning glory in the Blackmores' racing career of 40 years that enjoyed a series of highs and endured the most extreme of lows.

It is a career that is worthy of being recorded for posterity.

So here, told through a series of memorable episodes and anecdotes to mark the trainer's recent 95th birthday, is the story of Alan Blackmore and his wife Pat.

It is a story that highlights the crucial contributions of others, including their faithful, hardworking groom Emily Crossman and regular jockeys including Chris Honour.

And it is the story of a little racehorse with the heart of a lion, Cool Roxy – the Fakenham Favourite.

Cool Roxy and Chris Honour jump the last in Alan's birthday race

Alan with Fakenham Clerk of the Course David Hunter and the Princess Royal

Alan and Pat lead in an ecstatic Chris Honour and Cool Roxy after the race

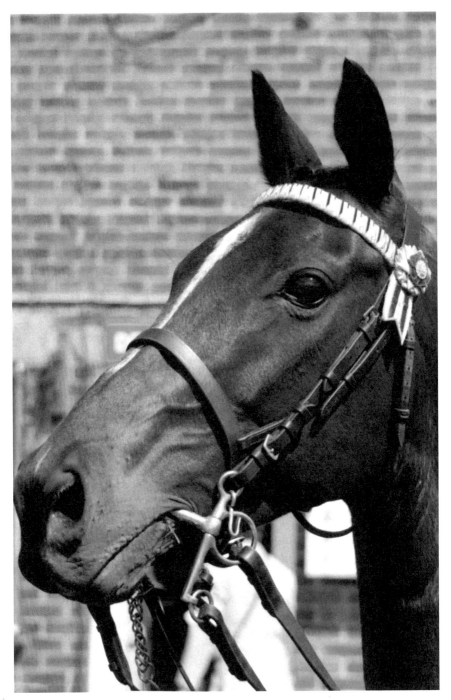

Cool Roxy

CHAPTER TWO

LOVE AT FIRST SIGHT

The first time I saw Cool Roxy run was also the first time I heard of Alan Blackmore. It was at Sandown Park, where I was an annual jumps member for 20 years, on Saturday 5th February 2005.

The race was the Agfa Hurdle, a Class A Listed race over two miles, and was primarily of interest because it featured the popular grey horse Rooster Booster, who had finished first and second in the last two Champion Hurdles at Cheltenham and was gearing up for a crack at another.

Rooster Booster was the odds-on favourite to win at 4-5. Cool Roxy, a pocket rocket of a horse, started as the rank outsider of the six runners, at odds of 100-1. The then eight-year-old hurdler had already run in 28 races, winning six, including five at Fakenham, but this 'Fakenham specialist' was hardly expected to trouble the great Rooster Booster here.

For 14 of the 16 furlongs, Cool Roxy led the field a merry dance. Ridden boldly from the front by Chris Honour, he was 50 lengths clear at the third hurdle.

Roxy sought to run the legs off the opposition whose riders, perhaps mindful of his tag as a specialist at a smaller course – and the fact that he was from the stable of a relatively un-known small trainer – allowed him his own way out in front.

The course commentator warned that the other riders might need to be careful as Roxy stretched away down the back of the hurdle track, near to where Sandown's famous Railway Fences stood, telling the February crowd: 'Cool Roxy is a good horse in his own right'.

However, two hurdles out, the field did indeed catch up with the runaway leader, and soon passed him.

Chris Honour calls this race 'the one that got away'. It was Roxy's first run back after his usual midwinter break and Chris is convinced that had the horse been what he called 'Fakenham-fit' they would have won that day.

But regardless of the final result, I had seen enough of Cool Roxy to be smitten. He had worn his heart on his sleeve and had not been afraid to take on the big boys – even away from his beloved Fakenham.

Having spotted on the racecard that Alan Blackmore trained locally to me, at Little Berkhamsted in Hertfordshire, I got in touch to discuss writing a feature on him for the local magazine I co-owned.

I soon discovered just how helpful and generous with their time both Alan and his wife Pat were; something that their friends have found over the years.

We did the interview in their home, surrounded by photographs and mementos of their time in racing, and, learning of my own interest in the National Hunt game, Alan insisted we stay in touch.

Over almost 20 years I got to know them both quite well, at one point even briefly riding out for Alan on a Sunday morning. I was too heavy and not good enough to be let anywhere near Cool Roxy, but I had the dubious pleasure of twice falling off his occasionally wayward stablemate Flaming Cheek. The second time came while cantering alongside Roxy and Emily Crossman and effectively (and understandably) put an end to my riding opportunity with Alan.

Despite this, I regularly trekked around the country to Fakenham and courses such as Huntingdon, Fontwell, Stratford and Worcester to see either Cool Roxy or Alan's other horses run. I went to point to points around the eastern region to watch Roxy compete at the age of 14, ridden by Emily, after he retired from racing under rules.

On one memorable morning I took a call at home at 6am from Alan, who was feeling unwell, asking if I could possibly drive the horsebox to Stratford as he had two runners there in the afternoon.

That drive, from Alan's yard in Hertfordshire via the M25 and M40, was the most nerve-wracking experience of my life. I had never driven a box before and I had two of Alan's thoroughbred racehorses on board, Pat alongside me and Emily in the back telling the two horses not to worry, everything would be OK, and apologising for the idiot driver who didn't seem to know when to brake at the right time. I still believe the imprints of my hands can be seen on the steering wheel today, so tightly was I holding it.

My association with the Blackmores and Cool Roxy even took me into the paddock at the Cheltenham Festival wearing an Owners' and Trainers' badge as Roxy took his chance in the Pertemps Final hurdle race in March 2006. Starting at 50-1, he finished a creditable ninth out of 24 runners.

All of these were wonderful and memorable experiences for a boy from a council estate in Harrow who didn't sit on a horse of any kind until after his 30th birthday.

Over the years I've been lucky enough to see some great moments on the racecourse, including Best Mate winning his third Gold Cup at Cheltenham. But nothing was more special than watching Roxy strut his stuff at Fakenham.

Just a mile round and set in the Norfolk countryside out-side the market town of the same name, this track was where Cool Roxy came alive. I have never shouted louder than when cheering him on there.

He raced at the course on 26 occasions, winning 11 times over both hurdles and fences – still more than any other horse. It was his backyard, and he was ready to repel all-comers, no matter what the name of the horse, trainer, jockey or owner.

'He could go round there blindfolded,' Alan Blackmore once told me. And do you know what, I think he was right.

Roxy even returned there, at the age of 18, to officially open the new Owners' and Trainers' Bar, which was named in his honour on 28th October 2015.

All sport has the capacity to make normally sensible people lose their heads at moments of great excitement – it can play with the emotions to a ridiculous extent.

But there is something special about the adrenalin that courses through your veins when you become emotionally invested in a brave and gutsy racehorse, particularly one you follow year-in, year-out, and even more so when you have been fortunate enough to be involved in a very small way with them.

And Cool Roxy was certainly one of those.

Alan and Pat Blackmore

CHAPTER THREE

MEET THE BLACKMORES

Alan Blackmore's path to training National Hunt racehorses was hardly a conventional one. After serving in the Royal Navy, he helped run the family business in London making dressmaking patterns before becoming a driving examiner and an exam invigilator.

But a love of horses had always run through Alan's blood. His grandfather, Arthur Greenwood, was a Master of Foxhounds near, of all places, Cheltenham – the home of jump racing.

Arthur was a wealthy gentleman farmer, owning around 400 acres of land, and when not riding to hounds or tending the land he found time to father seven daughters, the youngest of whom, Ruby Greenwood, was Alan's mother.

All seven of the Greenwood girls were sent to Cheltenham Ladies' College to put them on the right path but the patriarch's death in 1939 did not result in young Ruby being set up for life as might have been expected.

With six of his daughters, including Ruby, having married, Alan's grandfather decided to leave his entire estate to the one daughter – Daisy – who hadn't anyone else to look after her and the inheritance was enough for her to live out the rest of her days in luxury – staying in The Queens Hotel in Cheltenham!

Ruby Greenwood's marriage had been to Alan's father – Edward Philip Blackmore, known as Phil.

After leaving West Buckland School in Devon, Phil went straight into the Warwickshire Yeomanry regiment and found himself in Egypt in the First World War in 1914.

A 2nd Lieutenant, he led troops into battle at Gallipoli where the English officers were in charge of a group of young Australian conscripts, many of whom were slaughtered. Phil later told his son that he had effectively been ordered to lead his men to certain death.

Unlike many, Phil returned from Egypt, but his war was far from over. He joined the air force – then called the Royal Flying Corps – where he became a distinguished pilot flying the iconic Sopwith Camels and shot down a number of German planes.

Nicknamed Blacky in the RFC, Phil was himself shot down in 1917 and his plane dived straight into a bomb crater that had filled with water.

The Camel's wings broke up as the plane entered the water, but its nose ploughed into the soft clay underneath, something that stopped the cockpit being fully immersed.

As a result, Blacky survived the crash – another couple of inches in and he would almost certainly have drowned.

But when they heard he had been shot down, none of his pals believed he could have survived so back at base they began dividing up his kit between them, including his prized pair of gleaming new boots.

When a very much alive Blacky walked back into the mess the first thing he saw was a friend wearing them and immediately yelled out: 'Hey you – what the hell are you doing in my boots?!'

Such was the grim humour of those who fought.

It was after the war that Phil met Ruby Greenwood who, Alan recalls, was 'unusually full of get up and go' – and the only girl at Cheltenham Ladies' College who owned her own motorbike. As few women even drove a car back then, this was definitely out of the ordinary!

In 1923 Phil and Ruby had their first son, John, followed five years later by his brother, Alan Grenville Blackmore, who was born on 24th October 1928. The family settled in what were then the quiet and attractive suburbs of north London, living in Friern Barnet.

Like his grandfather, Alan's parents had horses and Alan learned to ride at an early age. In fact, being around horses was so natural to him that he regarded learning to ride a bike as far bigger an achievement than riding a horse.

Family holidays when John and Alan were still children involved taking a bungalow at Hillhead near Southsea, Hampshire, for a whole month of the summer every year from 1935 to 1939.

Despite the storm clouds of war again gathering, to the young Alan it was an idyllic time when the sun always seemed to be shining. Phil Blackmore hired a pony for Alan to ride and they also had a boat with an outboard motor so they could go out and enjoy the sea.

Not every experience was a happy one though.

One day, John had taken Alan out in the boat when Alan spotted something red bobbing in the sea and asked his brother if it was a buoy. They set off to find out but as they got nearer John realised it was the body of a woman wearing a red knitted bathing costume. She had drowned. The boys decided they had to do something, so Alan used a boathook to get hold of the woman's costume and they dragged the dead body slowly back to shore.

Back in Barnet, Alan had his own pony called Johnny who was kept with his parents' two thoroughbreds at a livery yard in nearby Cockfosters. Among the other families with horses at the yard were the Brooks-Wards, whose son Raymond would later go on to become the voice of showjumping on the BBC. Raymond and Alan would race their ponies through Trent Park, having the time of their lives.

Incredibly, when Alan's own son Christopher first learned to ride, it was on the same pony Johnny, who was still going strong well into his late 20s.

But the young Alan's love of speed wasn't confined to horses. In his late teens he had a motorbike which he used to ride, along with his friends, around the leafy lanes that characterised much of north London suburbia.

The girl who rode pillion with him back then in the late 1940s was called Pat Beresford, who lived in nearby Muswell Hill and who he had first met when he was 16 and she was 14 at a swimming pool in Finchley. Most of Alan's female friends had been banned from going out with him on his Triumph but Alan had always got on well with Pat's parents and recalls that they didn't mind her riding with him.

'They must have thought she was expendable!' he says.

But the danger of what they were doing was brought home to Alan when one of his friends was killed when he came off his bike. It taught him about the risks of speed – something that was to tragically haunt him in later life when he started training racehorses.

Pat was 'great fun'. A bright and vivacious girl, she loved dancing – in fact, she was still tap dancing well into her 80s.

She went to dance school and took part in a West End chorus line for several months, which went so well that she was asked to go on tour with the show. But while her father might have been content for her to ride on Alan Blackmore's motorbike, he wasn't having that and forbade it.

Pat's relationship with Alan continued even when he was conscripted and went to sea with the Royal Navy (his first choice, the RAF, was effectively closed to new recruits as it was such a popular option). When Alan came home on leave he would immediately head back to north London to meet Pat either at her home or Highgate Tube station.

Alan spent two and a half years in the Navy before returning home to help his brother John run the family business, Practical Fashions, which was based in Marchmont Street near Russell Square in London and made and sold dressmaking patterns.

Five years older than Alan, John had served in the Second World War in the RAF, flying Hurricanes and Spitfires. He was stationed in Burma for some time, often flying missions low over the jungle where Japanese soldiers were based.

The Japanese were renowned for their brutality towards enemy fighters and had a reputation for tying to a tree and bayonetting anyone they shot down and caught, so every pilot was given a service revolver with which to shoot himself if he survived being shot down, so he could avoid this gruesome fate.

One day, one of John's friends was shot down and his plane caught alight. At considerable risk to himself, John landed his own plane and managed to reach his friend, only to find that the pilot's legs were trapped and he was unable to get out of the cockpit. As the fire took hold, John could do nothing more to help him escape so he gave his doomed friend his own revolver so he could shoot himself rather than be killed by the fire.

It was something that stayed with him all his life. John survived the war and went on to marry Dorothy and the couple had two children, one son and one daughter. But the traumas of what he had seen contributed to him later becoming an alcoholic.

After the war the brothers ran the family business for a further four years but both had their respective interests which kept them away from the office at times. John continued to fly and Alan to ride horses. At one point John flew over Alan while he was out riding, prompting him to later ask his younger brother: 'What were you doing? I thought you were supposed to be at the office!'

Alan replied: 'Well, I thought you were in the office too!'

At the end of the 1940s, changing times led to the business's closure and the brothers sold the building in Marchmont Street. Alan went on to become a driving examiner, something which enabled him in his spare time to continue to pursue his love of speed – this time as a rally driver.

Alan and his navigator Malcolm Woodward raced all around the country and abroad, taking part in events including the Daily Express Rally and the RAC Rally, often winning their class. To begin with they drove a Ford Anglia, but things changed when Alan's father bought him a Triumph TR3, a car that was ahead of its time and which transformed the duo's racing fortunes. They went on to win the London Rally and Alan also took part in sports car racing at tracks including Snetterton, Goodwood, Brands Hatch and Silverstone for five years during the 1950s.

By this time, Alan and Pat had married, on 23rd June 1951, and drove their own Ford Popular to their honeymoon in the south of France. They had two children, both boys – Christopher in 1953 and Michael in 1955 – but this didn't stop them indulging in their joint love of dangerous sports. It was one of these that finally stopped Pat riding.

In the early 1960s she fractured her spine while skiing and had to be flown back to Whittington Hospital in Highgate where she was to spend six months. Alan was looking after their two boys at their home in Little Heath, just north of Barnet, taking them to school each day.

But though life was difficult, they both knew things could have been much worse – they were told that if the fracture had been just a quarter of an inch in a different place, Pat would have had to use a wheelchair for the rest of her life. As it was, she was told not to risk riding a horse again.

Alan, on the other hand, was still riding out regularly until he was 80 years old.

He only stopped after he had broken his hip in a fall for a second time, and his hospital consultant told him: 'You are going to end up in a wheelchair if you carry on riding. As it is, you will always need a walking stick from now on.'

Fortunately, Alan listened to the specialist's advice.

A young Alan on Johnny, his first pony

Alan (right) in his Royal Navy days

Alan at the Eastbourne Rally, 1958

Alan and Pat on their wedding day, 23rd June 1951

Christopher Blackmore about to 'leg up' his dad Alan before a point to point

CHAPTER FOUR

UNDER STARTER'S ORDERS...

Alan's love of speed and of riding was inevitably always going to lead in one direction – horse racing. He rode in point to points, buying his own horse called My Fortescue for £100. My Fortescue was a good horse but had a habit of finishing second or third – he made a noise when put under pressure. Nowadays, he would have been fitted with a tongue tie or given a breathing operation and would probably have won a few races, but he was great for Alan who said the horse 'gave me a lot of fun'.

One of Alan's most memorable point to point rides was not a win – or anything like one. He had fallen from his horse at Bishop's Stortford and, it transpired, had broken his arm. Not realising quite how badly he was hurt, he drove the horsebox to the hospital, was told the bad news, had the arm put in plaster – and then drove the horsebox home again afterwards!

Alan loved riding but he wanted to take his racing involvement in another direction as well, so he and his dad Phil went into racehorse ownership together.

They had their first runner with the trainer John Webber, though they had an unlucky start when the horse broke down in its first race at Ludlow. The Blackmores decided, in conjunction with the trainer, to retire it and find it a nice home rather than risk continuing to race.

Webber was keen to keep the Blackmores involved. He had half a dozen yearlings that he had bred himself and made them an offer: 'Pick one of these for £1,000 and leave it with me for a couple of years until it is ready to race.' So they did, picking out a lovely young horse called Foggerty.

But by the time Foggerty was due to have his first run, Phil Blackmore was stricken with cancer and on his death bed.

Then Webber's stable jockey John Buckingham picked up a ban and, the day before the race, the trainer told Alan they would have to withdraw.

However, knowing of Phil's parlous condition, Alan was determined Foggerty should take his chance so his father could know their horse had made it to the racetrack before he died.

At Webber's yard, the trainer's own son Anthony rode the

horse at home most days. Anthony was an amateur rider and had ridden in point to points but never under rules.

Alan suggested to the trainer that Anthony should ride the horse. It was the first example of something that would later become a trademark of Alan Blackmore – a willingness to give promising young riders a break.

The trainer wasn't convinced. 'The jockey's inexperienced, it would be his first ride under rules and it's the horse's first run – are you sure you really want to risk it?' he asked the fledgling owner. Alan said he did.

Foggerty, under young Anthony Webber, won easily at Leicester the next day by 12 lengths.

Alan dashed straight from the racecourse to the hospital to see his father and give him the good news. Despite the ravages of his cancer the smile on Phil's face was huge. 'I'm glad it's worked out so well,' he told his proud son, 'you'll have a lot of fun with him.'

Alan said: 'Someone was looking out for us.'

His father nodded.

The next morning, Phil Blackmore died.

Having now been both a jockey and a racehorse owner, Alan's next step was to go into training for himself. And he was determined to do it properly and find decent horses who would have a chance of winning a few races.

In 1970, he and Pat bought the home they have lived in ever since, down a quiet lane in the village of Little Berkhamsted near Hertford.

The house had its own small stable block next door and they installed a lunging pen and rented some grazing land behind it. For the first few years, Alan rode for fun around nearby Bayford Woods, while training his two point to pointers, My Fortescue and Arctic Sunrise, from his home.

In 1977, he applied for a permit, which allowed him to train his own National Hunt racehorses (as opposed to a commercial trainer who can be paid to train horses for other owners) and obtained use of a gallop. He was soon having runners, and winners, of which Silent Tango was the most successful.

Alan's groom at the time was Jacqueline Doyle, who was with the Blackmores for their first few years. She didn't do too badly afterwards either – becoming a trainer and winning the Winter Derby with Zanay in 2000. Her two children are the top international flat jockeys Sophie and James Doyle.

A decade later, Alan bought 25 acres of land just 100 yards up the road from his home to use as fields, then had a stable block and feed room built there so he had everything he needed on one site. He rented another 15 acres of land next door, giving him a total area of 40 acres to graze and work his horses.

This was to be the base for his training operation for the rest of his career, as he really started to make his mark with horses such as Arsonist, Silent Echo and Highland Flame, which all won multiple times in the late 1980s and 1990s.

With all of this going on at home, it was hardly surprising that both of the Blackmore sons had got the riding bug.

Like their father and grandfather, the boys were sent to West Buckland boarding school in Devon where Christopher, the eldest, found many of his friends were farmers' sons with horses.

He decided early on that he wanted to become a vet, specialising in horses. He later qualified at the Royal Veterinary College, where he also met his Norwegian future wife, Jenni. The couple had two children, Emma and Lars.

For a time, Christopher rode out for his dad, but realised that race riding was too much of a risk to his career so he took a full-time job at Park Veterinary Practice in Watford, where he later became a partner, earning himself a considerable reputation with horse owners around Hertfordshire and beyond.

His veterinary expertise became hugely important to Alan's training operation and his presence at the racecourse for decades was a constant support to his parents too.

Alan and Pat's younger son Michael, on the other hand, was determined to ride in races. This, ultimately, was a decision that was to end in tragedy.

Foggerty, the horse Alan owned in partnership with his father

The racehorses were initially based next to the Blackmores' back garden

Alan and Christopher riding out – long before helmets were compulsory!

Alan and Pat with Silent Tango, one of their early winners, at Towcester

A young Richard Dunwoody in the black and red silks of the Blackmores

CHAPTER FIVE

THE BOY DUN GOOD

If Alan Blackmore had a decent eye for a horse, he also had one for an up-and-coming jockey. Throughout his 40-year training career, he was never afraid to give a young rider a chance if he rated them.

Of course, this wasn't 100 per cent an altruistic move – as a shrewd trainer he knew the benefit that a good claiming jockey could bring. Less experienced riders are allowed to reduce the weight their horse is due to carry (called a 'claim') and if Alan could take 3, 5 or 7lbs of weight off his horse's back for a race he would do so – so long as the jockey was good enough.

Gee Armytage was one of those he championed – and we will see later how she repaid his faith in spades.

Chris Honour, who became known as Cool Roxy's rider,

was another who benefited from the patronage of the permit trainer, as did Marc Goldstein, while later on in his career, Alan was a big supporter of two very promising riding talents in Jack Quinlan and Tabitha Worsley.

One young rider Alan Blackmore spotted who went on to huge things within the sport was Richard Dunwoody.

The Northern Irishman subsequently rode for legends of racing including Captain Tim Forster, David Nicholson and Martin Pipe and became Champion Jockey three times.

He won the Grand National twice, the Gold Cup and the Champion Hurdle and rode some of the greatest horses jump racing has ever seen, including Desert Orchid and One Man – on both of which he won the King George VI Chase twice.

But Alan first saw Richard Dunwoody's potential when he watched him ride in a point to point, and the jockey was just a 19-year-old amateur when he had his first ride in the Blackmore colours, on Silent Echo in the Ouse Handicap Hurdle at Huntingdon on Boxing Day 1983. Despite his inexperience, Dunwoody brought Silent Echo home in first place, four lengths ahead of Haven Air and Brockley Belle.

But the stewards felt the young rider had drifted across his opponents after the last and called an enquiry.

The jockeys on the second and third horses were conditionals (apprentices) and were allowed to have their trainers speak for them. But as an amateur, Dunwoody had to speak for himself. The rules then assumed amateurs were well-educated, riding for fun and therefore able to represent themselves, while young professional jockeys were seen as working class and in need of someone better educated than them to speak on their behalf!

A clearly nervous Dunwoody was fed to the lions and the stewards not only reversed the placings but placed Silent Echo fourth – completely out of the prize money. Dunwoody was also banned for two days for careless riding.

One of the other trainers told Alan a few days later: 'Your lad didn't stand a chance. He was standing there trembling – I felt so sorry for the boy.'

Alan felt the stewards had got it wrong and was happy to support his rider, to the extent that he paired Dunwoody with Silent Echo again just five days later on New Year's Day at Windsor. They ran a fine race but two runs in five days proved slightly beyond Echo and they finished a gallant second.

Dunwoody may have gone from being a young rookie trembling in front of the stewards to one of the greatest riders National Hunt racing has ever seen, but he never forgot people like the Blackmores who helped him get started.

He name-checked them in his autobiography and invited them to his wedding and birthday parties. He also continued riding for them, whenever he could, well into the 1990s when he was at the height of his powers.

A focused and stylish Michael Blackmore in action over hurdles

CHAPTER SIX

THE DARKEST DAY

Racehorse trainers have to learn to accept the sad reality that a small percentage of horses in their care will be killed on the racetrack.

It is not an easy thing for any of us who love horses to reconcile ourselves to and different owners, trainers, jockeys and stable staff will each have different ways of doing so.

But losing a horse is one thing.

Losing a son to the sport you love is something else.

Michael Blackmore was a good rider and had his first ride in a point to point on a 12-year-old horse of his father's called Arctic Sunrise, which Alan himself had earlier ridden in points. The pair finished second.

In 1976, Michael was booked to ride Foggerty, the horse

Alan and his own father had bought and which was still trained by John Webber, in a hunter chase at Folkestone.

The pair were nicely positioned when the horse directly in front of them fell, bringing down Foggerty. Foggerty broke his shoulder and had to be put down.

The jockey was distraught, in floods of tears, and blamed himself for not plotting a wider course instead of following the horse in front. He vowed there and then to stop race riding, saying it was too upsetting.

He opted for a total change in life, going to catering college in Torquay where he was to meet his future wife, Frances.

They returned to Hertfordshire, settling in the village of Datchworth, and having a son, Philip, named after Alan's father, as Michael began a career as a catering manager.

But as the years passed, the urge to ride returned and, in 1983, seven years after the fatal fall of the family's much-loved Foggerty, he was back in the saddle again, and once more riding in National Hunt flat races ('bumpers') and amateur riders' hurdle races.

On 10th May 1986, Michael was booked to ride a young grey horse owned and trained by Alan called Silent Shadow at Market Rasen. The race was the second division of the Lincolnshire Amateur Riders' Maiden Hurdle.

The pair were up with the leaders early on in the race when Silent Shadow hit the third hurdle and came down.

As Michael lay on the ground he was kicked by another horse that came through.

From the grandstand at the racecourse, Alan and Pat could see that something was seriously wrong and they ran down the track to where their stricken son lay, being treated by St John Ambulance volunteers. At the time, there was no requirement for racecourses to have fully-trained paramedics on-site during racing – something that has since changed.

Michael was taken to Lincoln County Hospital but by the time he reached there it was too late. It turned out that a splinter of bone from a rib had punctured one of his lungs and his main artery. According to the website Jockeypedia, there is only one other incident of such an injury recorded.

At the age of 30, Michael Blackmore was dead, leaving behind not only his wife Frances and his 18-month-old son Philip, but his brother Christopher and the grieving parents whose own horse he had been riding when he fell.

Not surprisingly, the death of their younger son led to the Blackmores calling a halt to their training operation.

Eventually, it was their other son Christopher who encouraged them to resume. He could see they were not happy doing nothing and that they still had some nice horses in the yard. Nothing was going to bring Michael back and so, after six months, he persuaded them to start again.

During their time in racing, the Blackmores have had three moments of what you would have to call serendipity.

Foggerty winning the day before Alan's father died was the first.

Cool Roxy's record-breaking win on Alan's 80th birthday was another.

The middle one came at Warwick racecourse on 30th December 1987.

Warwick had kindly decided to stage a memorial race for Michael at their post-Christmas meeting. The Blackmore Amateur Riders' Handicap Chase was run for the first time just over 18 months after Michael's death and would take place for the next 10 years.

Alan was determined to have a runner in the first edition of the race and targeted Silent Echo at it – the same Silent Echo that Richard Dunwoody had done so well with.

Another promising jockey Alan had riding for him was Gee Armytage. She was one of the most successful of the early tranche of female jockeys who were blazing a trail years ahead of the days when the likes of Katie Walsh, Nina Carberry, Bryony Frost and Rachael Blackmore were to be rightly regarded as at least the equal of any man in the saddle.

And it was Gee Armytage who Alan turned to for the ride on Silent Echo.

So successful had the then 22-year-old become that she had

decided to make the jump from riding as an amateur to becoming a professional jockey, a move that would have ruled
her out of riding in the Blackmore memorial race.

But she selflessly delayed that switch in order to keep her
promise to the Blackmores and ride Silent Echo.

By now, Silent Echo was a 12-year-old and went off 2-1 second favourite behind Latin American at 7-4, ridden – just to
make things even more interesting – by Gee's brother Marcus
Armytage.

With half a mile of the two-and-a-half mile race to go, Marcus's mount was clear in the lead.

As they approached the final fence it was clear that Latin
American was tiring but Silent Echo looked set for a place at
best as he jumped the last still half a dozen lengths down.

As Latin American faltered, it was left to another challenger,
Lanacre Bridge, to surge into the lead.

But Silent Echo had clearly read the script.

Gee Armytage put her head down and somehow conjured
an incredible finish from her willing partner to sprint all the
way from the last to the winning post, roared on by an appreciative crowd who knew the story behind the race, taking
the lead with 100 yards to go and crossing the line in front of
Lanacre Bridge by just three quarters of a length.

In newspaper interviews after the race Gee told reporters:
'Having Marcus out in front was just the spur we needed – I

couldn't have him beating me! I would have gone professional a month ago but waited especially for this race, as the Blackmore family have done so much for me in the past.'

The tears flowed in the winner's enclosure afterwards as the Blackmores celebrated with their inspired jockey, and the Champagne flowed in the hours that followed too. Warwick had generously put a private room at the Blackmores' disposal for the day and provided food free of charge, requesting only that they paid for their drinks.

That was fine until a steady procession of well-wishers visited to pass on their congratulations, prompting Alan and Pat to buy each and every one of them a drink – pushing their bar bill up to around the £300 mark. Fortunately, the race prize money of £2,309.50 covered it.

But there are some things in life that you can't put a price on. And Silent Echo's poignant victory was one of them.

Gee Armytage after winning the race named in memory of Michael

Michael's widow Frances with Gee Armytage and the race winner's trophy

Pat and Alan Blackmore had a relaxed demeanour around their yard

CHAPTER SEVEN

CARPET FOR HURDLES

Alan Blackmore's approach to training racehorses was a simple one: to have happy horses, well looked-after. When racing, at whatever grade, they were always well-prepared and ready to give everything to win.

Compared with the larger professional yards, Alan's methods could be seen as being eccentric or idiosyncratic, but when you have smaller, more basic facilities you sometimes have to improvise and find your own way.

Directly outside his newly-built stable block were the fields where the horses would be out grazing together every single day – and 24 hours a day during the summer, when the Blackmores never raced their horses.

Here too, routine work could also be done on an all-weather

canter track that the horses used daily, building on the road work which took place on the lanes in and around Little Berkhamsted and surrounding villages on the outskirts of the county town of Hertford.

For fast work, Alan had his own six-furlong grass gallop and during the winter months he used an all-weather gallop near Enfield as well to get the horses spot-on to race. In later years, they would be boxed to schooling grounds at Newmarket to jump fences.

Back at home, in his own fields, Alan built a series of hurdles and fences to teach his horses to jump and give them practice. Here was a prime example of his 'make-do' approach – one that provoked a wry raised eyebrow from one BHA inspector who had come to check out the facilities, only to discover hurdles built from Formica and covered in stair carpet.

Not only was this soft covering designed to stop the horses hurting themselves if they dragged their hind legs through the jump but underneath it were cushions to make the experience even less painful!

The BHA inspector might have thought it was all a bit odd as he peered at the velveteen cushions underneath an old roll of Axminster, but he had to admit it worked.

Alan's career as a permit trainer has certainly had its unusual moments. One came after Richard Dunwoody's second race on Silent Echo on New Year's Day 1984 when the horse got away from the girl looking after him and escaped the Windsor course, galloping off along a dual carriageway in the direction of the M4.

The police were called because of reports of a loose horse on the road and as a patrol car drove past the course Alan flagged it down shouting 'Follow that horse!' and they pursued Echo towards Slough. Fortunately, it ended well as Echo ran off the road into a builder's yard and Alan was still in the police car when the report came over the radio that the horse was safe.

On 25th March 1995 Alan had to rent a horsebox to take the four-year-old Physical Fun to his first race, in a bumper at Newbury, because his own was having its MOT carried out.

Halfway along the M4, Alan's son Christopher, who was following in his car, caught up with the box and frantically signalled to his father to pull over.

Alan did so, only to find the roof had blown off and bits of it were scattered all over the motorway!

They managed to get Physical Fun to the races but decided they couldn't take him home in the box.

Luckily, fellow trainer Jenny Pitman kindly stepped in and offered to give the horse free board and lodgings for a few days until Alan was able to collect him in a box that wasn't open to the elements...

Physical Fun was a horse that stayed long in Alan's memory for another reason too. He had refused to race at Ascot in November 1997, something Alan put down to a young jockey being a little too enthusiastic with the whip in a previous race.

Alan took him to Sandown for his next run, two weeks later, on 5th December. The start for the two-mile six furlong race at the Esher course was a fair way from the grandstand and, knowing few people would see them, Alan and Pat had their own method of encouraging Physical Fun to begin the race.

No traditional flashing of whips for them – they took two water pistols down to the start and squirted them at the horse's backside until he finally set off!

Alan Blackmore began to get recognised more after he won the Permit Trainer of the Year award for the most winners in a National Hunt season three years in a row, which culminated in his being given the award on the podium in Cheltenham's famous winner's enclosure.

Meanwhile, Cool Roxy's record-breaking successes at Fakenham meant Alan was often listed in the racecard as the leading course trainer at the Norfolk track and he could barely walk a yard there without someone saying hello and wishing him luck.

But there were other racecourses where the trainer and his wife were less well known.

At Warwick on one occasion he was about to enter the Owners' and Trainers' Bar. By the side of the door was a board with the leading course trainers' names on it. In second place was Fred Rimell and in third was Martin Pipe. At the top, in first place, was Alan Blackmore.

As Alan went to go into the bar, an official on the door stopped him and said: 'I'm sorry sir but this bar is for owners and trainers only.' Alan got out his pass, pointed to his name on the board by the door, and said: 'I think the course's top trainer is allowed in, don't you?'

Alan and Pat's demeanour around their yard was very laid-back. Pat's little dog Patsy was always at the stables with them, flitting between the legs of the thoroughbred racehorses as though they weren't there.

At 4pm each day, Alan and Pat would simply open the gates from the fields to the stable block, shout 'Bed!' and these supposedly highly-strung, difficult to handle racehorses would come cantering or trotting up to have their feed on the yard and go into their boxes for the night.

And Pat's nonchalant approach was never seen to better effect in the secluded yard than in the middle of summer, when she had a habit of hosing down the horses wearing literally nothing but a baseball cap and a pair of old boots!

Permit Trainer of the Year. Christopher and Jenni Blackmore are on the right

Two of the Blackmore horses on the gallops

Some jumping practice at home

Happy horses in the Blackmores' fields in Little Berkhamsted

Chris Honour acknowledges the applause as Cool Roxy wins at Fakenham

CHAPTER EIGHT

COOL ROXY

One morning, Alan Blackmore told his wife he was going out to buy a fridge and came back with a racehorse. The pint-sized foal didn't cost him that much more than an American-style walk-in fridge either – at just under £1,500.

This was Cool Roxy, the little horse who was to take his elderly trainer to the Cheltenham Festival and gain legendary status as a cult hero in the unlikely surrounds of Fakenham.

Alan had seen Cool Roxy's dam, Roxy River, win once (when he'd also had his money on her) and remembered her as 'a really gutsy mare'.

So when her offspring came up in the Newmarket sale brochure he was instantly interested.

And when Pat thought Alan was in Currys seeking to improve their kitchen, he was in fact in the sale ring picking out his next steeplechaser.

Alan had got up early that morning and Pat, who wasn't feeling too well, had asked him: 'Where are you off to?'

'I'm going shopping,' said her husband.

'Well, we need a new fridge,' Pat told him.

'Of course, dear,' replied Alan, and headed off to get his horsebox.

Roxy was one of the early lots and, knowing that many people were there to look at two-year-olds they would be able to get on the track within a year or two, Alan was hopeful he might have a chance with the foal. He was the second bidder but was becoming dismayed when the auctioneer kept refusing to put down the hammer, continuing to seek more bids.

Alan, whose budget didn't include enough for both the horse and a new fridge to placate Pat, thought: 'I'm not going to get him.' But eventually the hammer went down in his favour. Perhaps the auctioneer had some inkling of the horse's potential because he looked the successful bidder in the eye and said: 'Well done sir!'

When Alan arrived home he had to admit he had come back with a foal rather than a new fridge, but a none-too-pleased Pat soon fell in love with Roxy, who went on to become the apple of her eye.

Roxy had been bred and sold by Mary Rimell, whose own family were steeped in racing history. Mary rang up Alan to congratulate him but admitted she was disappointed Roxy had only fetched £1,500 at the sale. Alan commiserated but told her: 'Don't worry, you'll get plenty of breeder's prize money when he starts winning.'

Mary never forgot that. She called Alan regularly whenever Roxy won a race to say: 'Thank you, I'm going to book another holiday now!'

But while the auctioneer, the breeder and the new owner-trainer all seemed confident that Cool Roxy was going to be something, Alan's vet son Christopher was less impressed when he first saw the stable's newest recruit, saying: 'You might win a pony race with him one day!'

However, like his mother, Christopher Blackmore was soon won over.

Though small at 15.2 hands high, Cool Roxy had perfect conformation and was the picture of an ideal horse both standing and when moving, something which contributed to his health and his longevity on the racecourse.

Over 10 years, Roxy ran 77 times under National Hunt rules and four times in point to points at the end of his career. He earned a total of £132,123 in prize money, of which £74,899 came from his 12 wins. His consistency was shown through his further 12 second place and 14 third place finishes.

But his future success was hardly obvious from the beginning. His first two races, at the end of 2001, in bumpers (National Hunt flat races) showed no promise at all to the casual observer. He finished 18th of 18 in his first racecourse outing, in the rarefied atmosphere of Sandown Park, and then 17th of 17 in his next, in the calmer waters of Huntingdon.

However, Alan liked his horses to have an educational introduction to racing, to get used to the hurly burly of large fields and to learn to enjoy what they were doing. He wasn't put off by his new charge's apparently slow start, and nor was his jockey. Chris Honour told the trainer: 'Don't worry about him – he'll be absolutely fine.'

Roxy's debut over hurdles, at, ironically enough, Fakenham, the course that was to become his spiritual home, ended in a crashing fall in March 2002. While the big names were taking their chances at the Cheltenham Festival on the same day, Alan Blackmore's big hope was taking the only tumble of his entire career.

Until the fall, it had been a promising run. Roxy was in fourth place (14 ran), despite having started at odds of 66-1, and was approaching the final hurdle of the two-mile race when, in Alan's own words, 'he clouted the last, did a 'loop de loop' and cartwheeled right over.' But the trainer recalls: 'He got up straight away and shook himself. You never want to see your horse fall but in this instance it was almost a blessing in disguise. I actually think it was the making of him.'

Alan continued to run Roxy regularly throughout 2002, when he was ridden every time bar one by Chris Honour, but it was to be another seven months and six races before he was to experience victory for the first time. Of course, it was at Fakenham, the first of his 11 wins at the Norfolk track.

Having finished in fourth place for four consecutive races, he finally got his head in front in a hurdle race over two miles on 24th November 2002. Roxy had led for most of the race before being headed at the second last hurdle. But he showed the guts and determination that were to become his trademark by rallying and getting back up to beat the 5-4 favourite Take Heed by just half a length at odds of 9-1.

Cool Roxy had arrived and Fakenham, though it probably didn't realise it then, had a new hero.

Although, inevitably, Cool Roxy became known as a Fakenham specialist, he still ran with great credit elsewhere.

That one 'away win' was on 14th November 2004 over hurdles in Sussex at Fontwell (another idiosyncratic course, with an unusual figure of eight configuration), but his career over the smaller obstacles also saw him finish in the places at Grade One racecourses Newbury and Ascot as he rose from his first official rating of 78 up through the ranks to a mark that regularly hovered around 130 (he went on to reach a career-high of

133 over fences in March 2009). His sheer consistency earned him a crack at the Cheltenham Festival, where Roxy took his place in the Pertemps Final, a handicap hurdle race over three miles, on 16th March 2006.

Now, even non-racing fans know how big a deal the Cheltenham Festival is – it's jump racing's Olympics, but it comes round every year. Back in 2006 it was no less important to the racing fraternity, and for a then 77-year-old permit trainer from Hertfordshire, simply having a horse good enough to be a runner there was no mean achievement.

As the Blackmores stood with their friends in the paddock before the race, with their stable star taking his place among the 24 runners trained by the likes of Martin Pipe, Paul Nicholls, Jonjo O'Neill and Alan King, Alan couldn't help but pinch himself.

It was a huge day for jockey Chris Honour too – his first ride at the Cheltenham Festival.

Chris recalled: 'I was absolutely determined to take it all in –I didn't know if I'd ever get another chance to ride at the Festival. The start of the Pertemps is by the Best Mate enclosure so you can see all of the stands in front of you. I deliberately took myself away from the other horses, and looked up at the grandstands filled with 60,000 people. I just thought 'that's pretty cool'. I remember it more than any of my other rides there, it was brilliant.'

Fortunately, Cool Roxy wasn't overawed. Sent off at odds of 50-1 he ran a fine race, being up among the leaders until three out when he was finally outpaced. He still stayed on well after the last to eventually finish in ninth place, only 13 lengths behind the Irish-trained winner, Kadoun.

By now Alan realised that Roxy's increasingly lofty rating was going to make it difficult for him to win races over hurdles, and Chris Honour was winning more races too so his claim was also reducing.

Having taken 7lbs off Roxy's back when he first rode him, Chris's claim was at this stage down to just 3lbs, meaning Roxy was having to shoulder bigger burdens through a combination of this and his own consistency, which saw the handicapper refuse to drop him much in the weights.

So, at the unusually late age of nine years old, Cool Roxy was prepared for his first race over steeplechase fences.

It was a bit of a gamble, especially bearing in mind Roxy's size, but Chris Honour said: 'When we first took him to The Links at Newmarket to school him over fences, I remember the gallops man watching him and just saying 'Wow!'

'Roxy was phenomenal – it was as though he was on springs.'

Just two months after his Cheltenham Festival experience, and having finished third in two more hurdle races since, Roxy had his first taste of the bigger obstacles, on 21st May

2006 at – of course – Fakenham. Over the by now shorter than ideal distance of just two miles, he ran his usual brave race from the front to beat Evan Williams's Serbollini by five lengths, with two rivals from the larger stables of Oliver Sherwood and Paul Nicholls having failed to navigate the Fakenham fences. There was no such trouble for Cool Roxy, and Chris Honour brought him home to appreciative cheers from the knowledgeable Norfolk crowd who had come to see their little hero take on the larger obstacles for the first time.

He was already a standing dish at the track, having won five times over hurdles by then. His sixth win, this time over fences, was to prove just a taster for what was to follow as he was to go from being a prolific winner to a bona-fide local hero and record breaker.

Whether it was his bold, never-say-die, front-running style, his small size, his pensioner trainer with his still sprightly wife, or his unassuming jockey... whatever it was, the Norfolk racegoers took Cool Roxy and everyone associated with him to their hearts.

Fakenham is not the easiest course to ride: left-handed, it's just a mile round, it's undulating and has a short run-in after the final fence which is jumped just after you enter the straight. But it suited Cool Roxy as nowhere else did. And Cool Roxy suited the regulars who flocked to Fakenham – many just to see him run. David Hunter, the long-serving and excellent Clerk of the Course and Chief Executive at Fakenham, spoke about Roxy to the Racecourse Association in 2021 for its Local Legends series, which featured horses that attained legendary status at racecourses around Britain, collated to mark that year's National Racehorse Week.

David said: 'Cool Roxy had a huge following at Fakenham. He was the most fantastic horse, a neat and tidy jumper with the heart of a lion.

'When he ran at Fakenham the gate would increase, he was so popular. I have never heard such cheers and roars from Fakenham's enthusiastic and knowledgeable crowd as when Roxy won. He was a lovely horse with a kind eye and often won best turned out. It was a real privilege to be Clerk during his period of Fakenham dominance. My only regret is that I never sat on him!'

Cool Roxy continued to run well at Fakenham and elsewhere throughout 2006 and 2007 and ended up back in Norfolk on Friday 16th March 2007, the same day as that year's Cheltenham Gold Cup, which was won by the Paul Nicholls-trained chaser Kauto Star.

The Fakenham racegoers watched on the big screens as Kauto memorably won the first of his two Gold Cups in the race which went off at 3.15pm, just as the horses were circling the paddock for the Tim Barclay Memorial Chase at 3.30pm.

Five and a half minutes after the off time, Chris Honour and Cool Roxy jumped the final fence to romp to an eight-length victory over an old rival, Herecomestanley trained by Milton Harris, prompting course commentator Derek 'Thommo' Thompson to ecstatically cry as the winner crossed the line: 'Who needs Kauto Star? Here's our very own Gold Cup winner... Cool Roxy!'

Thommo was never understated. But he caught the mood of the cheering Fakenham thousands perfectly that day.

By now, Roxy's dominance and popularity at Fakenham were in danger of scaring some owners and trainers off from running their horses against him at the course.

Alan said: 'They all tried to beat Cool Roxy at Fakenham, but he'd beaten horses trained by the likes of Paul Nicholls and Nicky Henderson there. We weren't afraid of anyone.'

One trainer, aware of just how strong Roxy was at the course, had tried to dissuade one of his owners, who was keen to go there for one particular race, from doing so.

He warned him: 'We shouldn't go – he won't beat Cool Roxy at Fakenham.' The owner was aghast at the idea that they couldn't beat a horse with 'a geriatric trainer who only had a few horses', and he insisted that they run.

Alan recalled: 'We were stood near the owner and his friends in the stand and as their horse got close to Roxy approaching the last they were getting excited, thinking they were about to win. I stood there and shouted 'Go get it Roxy!' and he motored away from the last to win nicely. The Fakenham crowd was going mad.'

The beaten trainer said to Alan afterwards: 'I did tell him, but he wouldn't believe me!'

Mixing hurdling and chasing, Cool Roxy continued to run ultra-consistently, including in a hurdle race at Kempton Park in November 2007 when he almost ran down Nicky Henderson's heavily-eased Chomba Womba to finish within three-quarters of a length. Roxy was actually ahead just after the winning post – beating that year's Champion Hurdle third Mobaasher into second place.

That was one of no fewer than four second place finishes in a 12-month period, including two at Fakenham, where the crowd's love affair with their hero showed no signs of flagging.

And never was that affair celebrated more wildly than on 24th October 2008 – the day of Alan Blackmore's 80th birthday – as recounted in this book's opening chapter.

Keen to give something back to the racecourse that had given him so many great days, Alan decided to sponsor the 3m chase on the card, which was named the Alan Blackmore Birthday Handicap Chase, and he entered Cool Roxy to run.

It proved to be an unforgettable day. First, Alan had to be on his best behaviour when he and Pat had lunch with HRH the Princess Royal before the race.

As it turned out, trying to remember his Ps and Qs was the most stressful part of Alan's day.

The now 11-year-old Roxy led from the start in trademark style before sauntering to a 24-length victory – his first win in a year – and becoming the winning-most horse at Fakenham in the process. Even his usually cool jockey Chris Honour celebrated as he crossed the line in front of the packed stands.

The crowd, it is fair to say, went bananas.

Age will eventually catch up with any racehorse, no matter how honest and gallant. Cool Roxy went on to win one more race, his 11th at Fakenham and 12th overall, on 27th February 2009 at the grand old age of 12, and continued to run his heart out all the way through to what was intended to be his final race under rules, on 23rd May 2010, at Fakenham, in the Rex Carter Memorial Handicap Chase.

After he had finished a brave third, beaten just four and a half lengths by Dead or Alive, a horse of Tim Vaughan's six years younger than him, Cool Roxy was retired. Alan let the racecourse officials know in time for Roxy to be paraded around the paddock where he received a rousing and prolonged reception from the crowd when the news was announced.

Roxy had won more than £131,000 in prize money, prompting Pat Blackmore, when asked what she thought of that by the Racing Post, to reply: 'Well, I don't know where the money has gone – I haven't had a new pair of shoes in years!'

But though his trainer knew Roxy's best racing days were behind him, the horse didn't. So keen did he remain at home that Alan decided to give him a swansong in the point to point field the following winter, offering the opportunity for his groom Emily Crossman to ride him in races, something she was hugely grateful for, calling it 'an amazing experience'.

Together, they raced four times on the East Anglian circuit, finishing fourth, third and second twice, including by just two lengths in their last race at Marks Tey in Essex on 2nd April 2011.

Yet still the final chapter of the Cool Roxy story was not written. He was by now 14 but, because he had run with such enthusiasm in the points, Alan gave him one more last hurrah – back at Fakenham with a new young jockey – the hugely promising Jack Quinlan – on board.

As always, Roxy did his best, but just two weeks after running at Marks Tey, younger legs prevailed and he finished a never-threatening fourth of seven runners.

It meant his final race record at Fakenham was 26 runs, 11 wins, six seconds, three thirds and four fourths, plus one unseated rider and one fall – in that very first hurdle race.

Of his total 77 races, Chris Honour rode him in 70, winning 11 of them, including the lone victory away from Norfolk, at Fontwell. The other rider to win on Roxy (note this if you attend a quiz night at Fakenham!) was Andrew Glassonbury.

Chris said of the horse he will forever be associated with as a rider: 'He had so much scope and so much talent. At our own level he was our Champion Hurdler and Gold Cup winner all rolled into one. He took us to so many places and we had so many great days with him – it was unreal.

'If it wasn't for Cool Roxy I would have struggled to carry on riding at times. My association with him was what kept me going when things were tough. He was such a big part of my life and I will forever be grateful to him and the Blackmores. They are brilliant people.'

Now, finally, almost 10 years after making his inauspicious debut in a bumper at Sandown Park and having gone on to become the winning-most horse in the history of Fakenham racecourse, the Cool Roxy era really was over.

Alan gifted Roxy to Emily Crossman. Emily, like Alan and Pat, was devoted to Roxy. She had joined the Blackmores in 2003 and worked for them for a decade. She had first met them after riding a horse for somebody she knew over Christmas 2002, when she had gone for a hack with a local couple called Jill and Terry Love. They had got chatting during the ride and Jill and Terry had asked Emily what she wanted to do.

When Emily said she hoped to work in racing they told her they knew a trainer nearby and would pass on her number to him. A couple of weeks later, Alan Blackmore called her and invited her over for a trial to ride out. The horse she rode round the villages that morning was Cool Roxy.

Recalling that chance beginning, Emily said: 'I owe a lot to the Blackmores – and to Jill and Terry Love.'

On her time with the Blackmores, Emily said: 'They are an inspiration in themselves. They would turn up every day, showing their dedication, love and commitment to the sport, even after suffering more than their fair share of hardship.

'They were quite unusual – the schooling fences were some-what makeshift when I started, though we did improve them a bit over the years, but the proof that their methods worked was evident – no-one could deny that Alan's horses always jumped well on the track.

'Alan was very passionate about not overdoing things. He was realistic about the demands of racing but he was always kind to his horses. And he was still riding out regularly in his 70s – despite one of his legs being basically filled with metal!

'His son Chris used to call me regularly to get to know more about the horses and how they were going. All in all, they were a very dedicated family.'

Emily gave Cool Roxy a fruitful second chapter after racing. She said: 'We did showjumping, cross country and dressage and generally had a good time. On one occasion I took him on a sponsored ride with friends but we had to leave them behind as every time he saw a horse in front of him he felt we had to go and get past it! Needless to say, we got round quicker than most! Cool Roxy committed to everything he did; he was always kind, honest, genuine and a pleasure to have around.'

A particular highlight of their time together came on 28th October 2015, when they returned to Fakenham to open the new Owners' and Trainers' Bar which had been named after Roxy, who was to be the guest of honour.

The opening took place an hour before that day's first race. Roxy looked an absolute picture and was determined to be the centre of attention. There was no standing by politely while the humans carried out the official opening – Cool Roxy, with Emily by his side, did it himself.

Emily recalled: 'It was a very special and memorable occasion and friends and family came from all around. Fakenham never failed to make us welcome – from the staff to the regular racegoers, everyone had a genuine love for horse racing.

'We used to sometimes catch up with a crowd after the first race, eat homemade sandwiches and drink port while chatting about that day's racing.

'For the opening, David Hunter asked me if Roxy would go

into the bar and then exit through the red tape. I said 'absolutely – he'll pour the pints if you ask him nicely!'

'Roxy was the perfect gentleman, and luckily he didn't leave a mess behind.'

Afterwards, Alan admitted: 'I was a little nervous when Roxy headed into the bar, but he was clearly impressed as once he entered he didn't want to leave! It was a typically thoughtful gesture of the racecourse team to think of me and Roxy with their new facility and it's wonderful to think that he will be remembered by so many there for years to come.'

Pat Blackmore was also delighted, greeting the gelding's memorable 'a horse walked into a bar' moment by saying: 'Cool Roxy's like me – he likes a drink!'

The Cool Roxy story finally came to an end in 2017 when, at the age of 20, he sadly succumbed to colic.

The little horse had become an unlikely folk hero. He had taken his permit-holding trainer to the Cheltenham Festival and won him almost 100 times what he had cost him as a foal.

More importantly, he had won the hearts of thousands, including Pat Blackmore, the wife who had thought her husband was going out one morning to buy a fridge, only to see him come back with a racehorse.

Christopher Blackmore, Chris Honour and Cool Roxy at Cheltenham

In more familiar surroundings – inspecting the first at Fakenham

Emily Crossman parading Cool Roxy back at Fakenham after his retirement

That winning feeling at Fakenham

Amateur jockey Jason Newbold winning on Flaming Cheek

CHAPTER NINE

FLAMING CHEEK

Sharing the yard with Roxy during his heyday was Flaming Cheek. Alan had high hopes for Cheeky, though a succession of injuries curtailed his achievements.

Jockey Chris Honour called him 'hard as nails' and said he would have won a lot of races if he hadn't been so unlucky with injuries. A sharp horse who often had to be mounted on the track to stop him boiling over during the preliminaries, Flaming Cheek had been well named. He also, inadvertently, almost got Alan into trouble over a large winning bet...

Cheeky was lucky to still be on the racecourse. At the end of May 2004, he won very nicely by 13 lengths in a hurdle race at Stratford ridden by the amateur jockey Jason Newbold. A week later he had a nasty schooling accident at Newmarket when his tendon was sliced into. The vets advised Alan that he might have to be put to sleep, but Alan was determined to save him, even if it meant him just going to be a hack for someone and not seeing a racecourse again.

Some excellent veterinary treatment saw Cheeky return home after six weeks at Newmarket. For month after month, he was allowed to just be a horse and it was some 18 months before he was sound and starting to work again.

Alan, with his vet son Christopher's eventual approval, finally got him back on the track after a 664-day absence.

Flaming Cheek ran six times between March and November 2006, the last of which saw him finish a close-up fourth at Towcester with Chris Honour on board.

The day after that race, Alan found some heat in one of the horse's legs and he was off the track for another 469 days before returning in March 2008. He ran without any great promise four times before a stand-out effort that December at Fontwell when he finished second at 66-1, which proved that the old ability was still there.

A short winter break followed before two midfield runs in the spring put him spot-on for a race on 24th March 2009 at Southwell when he would also encounter his favoured better ground for the first time in a while.

Aware that this injury-prone horse had had a lot of time

off the track, the bookmakers gave him little chance, and he could be readily backed at 20-1 when the prices were chalked up. Off-course, in the betting shops, you could get 33-1. Suddenly, the price in the shops began to tumble to 28-1, then 25-1 and further still.

At Southwell, punters latched on as the on-course announcer reported 'a massive gamble on Flaming Cheek'.

As the tapes rose, Cheeky's price had contracted to 8-1.

Chris Honour rode his usual calm race, holding his horse up early on before making steady progress through the field and taking the lead three from home, eventually winning by three lengths.

Afterwards, the stewards called the trainer in for a chat and asked if he had any observations about the betting patterns, which led Alan to brandish his £10 each-way slip from the Tote, saying: 'Well I don't think this was responsible!'

It later transpired that a policeman friend of Alan's, who had phoned him to ask how Cheeky was going at home, had had a whip-round among his colleagues at Scotland Yard and got together £600, which rewarded them richly at the odds of 33-1 he was able to get. It was this bet that had started the gamble.

The horse Flaming Cheek beat into second place that day was called Badly Bruised. Which must have been how the bookies felt too.

Marc Goldstein and Occasionally Yours after their first win at Huntingdon

CHAPTER TEN

AFTER ROXY

No matter how big or small a trainer is, the moment a flagship horse is retired or leaves the yard, it leaves a big stable to fill. When you are as successful as Paul Nicholls or Nicky Henderson, there is a good chance you'll have one in the pipeline to follow on from Kauto Star or Denman, or Sprinter Sacre or Altior.

But when you are Alan Blackmore, an octogenarian permit trainer with two or three horses, finding one to replace Cool Roxy was always going to be a challenge.

Despite the heavy odds against unearthing another good one, Alan was not put off.

He had always preferred to buy his horses young, so he could teach them his own way of doing things from the start, and he bought a couple of youngsters who he named after the fashion of Roxy – Cool Contender and Cool Chief. Both were nice horses to ride but sadly neither cut it on the racecourse.

So, as the end of his training career approached, Alan was realistic enough to buy some slightly older horses already in training elsewhere that he could get on the track straight away.

One he bought as a six-year-old, and almost won with, was Monroe Park. Monroe finished second twice at Fakenham but, unusually for a Blackmore horse, fell several times in his five seasons in the black and red.

However, another proved to be a roaring success. This was the brilliantly named hurdler Occasionally Yours (he'd been owned by a syndicate) and he became the yard's final flagbearer after the retirement of Cool Roxy.

His stable name was Basil – and hearing Pat Blackmore call him in from the field for his dinner had more than a touch of Sybil Fawlty about it. He was a lovely, narrow animal who came to the Blackmores with a bit of a reputation for being difficult when he was tied up on the yard.

But the couple's laid-back and natural approach soon sorted out that problem. Alan explained: 'He used to go mad when tied up. So every time we tied him up we did it with baling twine, so he could break it if he wanted to. Then we gave him a Polo. If he pulled away and broke the twine, I'd just say 'oh you silly boy' and tie him up again. He soon worked out that he could get away if he wanted to but if he stayed there he'd get a Polo!

'He also had 40 acres including an area of sand to roll around in. He realised he quite liked it here. He was a lovely horse and he went on to repay us 100 times over.'

When Alan bought him in September 2010 Occasionally Yours had already run 13 times, winning once for Nigel Hawke.

In his final race for the trainer, he had been ridden by the record-breaking Champion Jockey A P McCoy, though even The Champ's assistance could only help him finish sixth.

In his first run for Alan that October, with another of his trusted jockeys Marc Goldstein up, Occasionally Yours ran away with a two-mile hurdle at Huntingdon, winning by eight lengths. Cool Roxy may have retired, but Alan knew he had another decent one to go to the races with.

Like Roxy, Basil became a model of consistency. As another of his jockeys, Jack Quinlan, once told me at Fontwell: 'He knows his job, this one.'

In his first year with Alan, Occasionally Yours ran no fewer than nine times, winning twice, finishing second once and third three times. Among those runs were two at Sandown and one at Cheltenham. At Sandown, ridden both times by Jack Quinlan, he finished third and then second with two fine efforts.

The first of those, on the high-profile Imperial Cup card just days before Cheltenham on 12th March 2011, was in the European Breeders' Fund National Hunt Novices Hurdle Final.

Unheralded, he went off at 40-1 but an absolute masterclass of a ride by Jack Quinlan, who was still an amateur claiming 7lbs at the time, had him in the vanguard the whole way and he was beaten by only three-and-a-half half lengths in the end by Skint, trained by Nicky Henderson and ridden by Barry Geraghty.

Jack's ride was highly praised on Channel 4 Racing afterwards by an all-time great, that superbly stylish and outspoken seven times Champion Jockey John Francome.

Just over a month later the pair came close again back at Sandown, this time at the Whitbread Gold Cup meeting, finishing just three lengths second to Sandown specialist Gary Moore's horse Sunley Peace in the bet365 Handicap Hurdle.

Basil's first 12 months with the Blackmores ended as it had begun – with a win. At Worcester, with Jack Quinlan again riding, he beat Cockney Trucker to claim victory under a welter burden of 11st 12lbs.

Occasionally Yours continued to run consistently well wherever he went, finding Sandown and Fontwell particularly to his liking. Alan would have loved him to follow in the hoofsteps of Roxy, so took him regularly up to Fakenham, but the course didn't really play to his strengths.

Though never disgraced, it took him five years and 15 runs at the Norfolk track before he recorded the first of his two wins there, in May 2015.

On that occasion he was ridden by Tabitha Worsley, another talented, young 7lb claimer that Alan was putting up regularly, with Jack Quinlan now deservedly getting rides for other trainers including Lucy Wadham and Amy Murphy.

Tabitha also rode Basil to victory at Huntingdon on 14th November 2017 and was set to follow up back at Fakenham a week later, but broke her back in a fall at Ludlow.

Jack Quinlan stepped in for the ride at Fakenham, and the pair also won. By now, the horse was 13 and the trainer 89 – and it proved to be the final career victory for them both, with Alan heralding it as 'a great day for a geriatric trainer and a geriatric horse'.

In all, Occasionally Yours won nine races in the Blackmore colours, including a three timer in 2015, rising to a career high official handicap rating of 132, just 1lb below the highest rating ever given to Cool Roxy.

Tabitha Worsley recovered to have her finest moment so far winning the Foxhunters Chase at Aintree aboard Top Wood over the Grand National Fences in 2019 – 17 months after breaking her back. She was Alan's most regular rider for the last five years of his career and, like her predecessors, she never let the Blackmores down.

Marc Goldstein getting the best out of Occasionally Yours

Connie Taylor, a good friend of the Blackmores, with Pat and Cool Contender

Pat, Alan, Basil, groom Fin Hemmings and Tabitha Worsley win at Huntingdon

Jack Quinlan, praised by John Francome, showing his style on Monroe Park

Christopher Blackmore was by his father's side throughout his training career

CHAPTER ELEVEN

THE FINAL FENCE

The last horse Alan trained was called Cocker. He was a full brother to the high-class flat stayer Brown Panther, bred and owned by Michael Owen and trained on the flat by Tom Dascombe. Alan bought him in 2015.

Like Occasionally Yours before him, Cocker benefited from some trademark Blackmore care.

Jack Quinlan had ridden him in a race and reported back that Cocker had seemed reluctant to go through the gap between runners which had opened up, and it turned out that he seemed a bit scared around other horses.

Alan said: 'We believe he'd been kept in a paddock by himself before and perhaps wasn't that used to being around other horses. So we gave him some time and put him out in a big

93

field with the others, where he could have his own space when he wanted it, but could also get used to being part of a group. After a few months he was a different horse.

'In April 2016 we went to Fontwell with Cocker and Occasionally Yours, with Tabitha Worsley riding both. Occasionally Yours ran well to finish third at 16-1, not beaten far. Then it was Cocker's turn. He went off at 100-1 but was well placed when suddenly the gap came – and he went through it! He finished a fast-closing third – a bit further and he'd have won.'

But despite this breakthrough, that race proved to be Cocker's best run over hurdles and the dream of a win with him was not to be realised.

Occasionally Yours had five runs in 2018 at the age of 14, finishing third in his final outing at Fakenham, but it was Cocker who ran in what turned out to be Alan's last race as a trainer.

This was also at Fakenham, on 7th May 2019, though there was to be no fairytale ending, as Cocker was pulled up under Tabitha Worsley at 100-1.

Around this time, Alan's first son, Christopher, who had always been such an important part of the Blackmores' set-up, received the devastating news that the cancer he had been diagnosed with two years earlier was terminal, and it was this that made Alan decide the time had finally come to retire from training. He was 90 years old and officially the country's oldest active trainer.

He explained: 'Without Christopher helping us, we didn't want to go on training. His veterinary skills were absolutely invaluable, checking horses we wanted to buy and then looking after them. It would have been impossible to carry on.'

Alan retired Cocker and found him a good home with a woman who rode him out alongside her ten-year-old son on his pony.

Two years later, Christopher Blackmore, acclaimed vet, keen tennis player and, while he was undergoing cancer treatment, the author of a children's book written with his two granddaughters in mind, died on 9th June 2021 at the age of 68.

Alan and Pat had now seen both their sons pre-decease them. After Michael's tragic death, they had somehow found the strength to carry on in racing, with the help and support of Christopher, and achieve three more decades of success.

Three decades which brought them and the wider racing family, who hold this remarkable couple close to their hearts, so much joy.

This is the couple whose skill, horsemanship and dedication (along with some less conventional tools of old carpet, water pistols and Polos) brought the best out of all their horses.

And, of course, the couple who gave us the unforgettable Cool Roxy – the Fakenham Favourite.

Cool Roxy and Emily Crossman open Fakenham's Owners' and Trainers' Bar